insight text guide

Scott Hurley

A Lesson Before Dying

Ernest J. Gaines

insight®

▶ innovative ▶ engaging ▶ evolving

First published in 2002, reprinted in 2016, 2020.

Insight Publications Pty Ltd
3/350 Charman Road
Cheltenham VIC 3192
Australia
Tel: +61 3 8571 4950
Fax: +61 3 8571 0257
Email: books@insightpublications.com.au

www.insightpublications.com.au

National Library of Australia Cataloguing-in-Publication entry:
    Hurley, Scott.
    A lesson before dying, Ernest Gaines.
    For secondary and tertiary students.
    ISBN 9781920693077
    1. Gaines, Ernest J., 1933–. Lesson before dying. I. Title. (Series: Insight Text Guide)
    813.54

Other ISBNs:
    9781922525178 (digital)
    9781922525185 (bundle: print + digital)

Cover design by Gisela Beer, based on a concept by The Modern Art Production Group

Printed in Australia by Ligare

contents

CHARACTER MAP

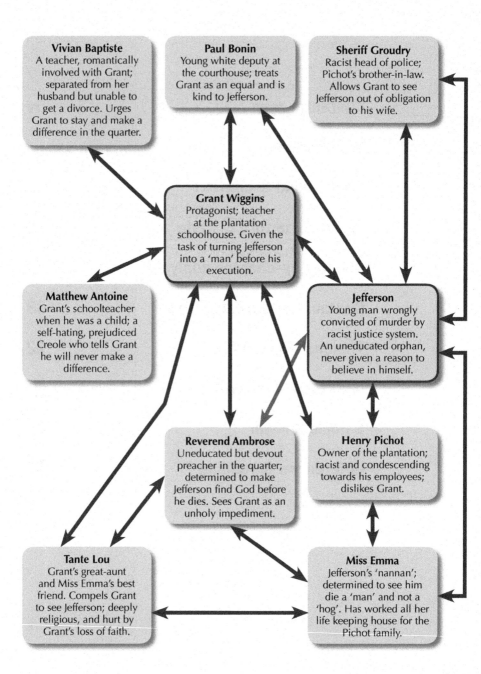

Vivian Baptiste
A teacher, romantically involved with Grant; separated from her husband but unable to get a divorce. Urges Grant to stay and make a difference in the quarter.

Paul Bonin
Young white deputy at the courthouse; treats Grant as an equal and is kind to Jefferson.

Sheriff Groudry
Racist head of police; Pichot's brother-in-law. Allows Grant to see Jefferson out of obligation to his wife.

Grant Wiggins
Protagonist; teacher at the plantation schoolhouse. Given the task of turning Jefferson into a 'man' before his execution.

Matthew Antoine
Grant's schoolteacher when he was a child; a self-hating, prejudiced Creole who tells Grant he will never make a difference.

Jefferson
Young man wrongly convicted of murder by racist justice system. An uneducated orphan, never given a reason to believe in himself.

Reverend Ambrose
Uneducated but devout preacher in the quarter; determined to make Jefferson find God before he dies. Sees Grant as an unholy impediment.

Henry Pichot
Owner of the plantation; racist and condescending towards his employees; dislikes Grant.

Tante Lou
Grant's great-aunt and Miss Emma's best friend. Compels Grant to see Jefferson; deeply religious, and hurt by Grant's loss of faith.

Miss Emma
Jefferson's 'nannan'; determined to see him die a 'man' and not a 'hog'. Has worked all her life keeping house for the Pichot family.

INTRODUCTION

Ernest J Gaines was born in 1933 in Oscar, Louisiana. He moved to San Francisco in 1948 to join his parents, after being raised by an aunt on a plantation similar to the one described in *A Lesson Before Dying*. The winner of numerous literary awards, Gaines is considered to be at the forefront of the African-American and the Southern literary traditions. His eight novels are all set in the rural Louisiana of his birth.

A Lesson Before Dying is the story of two young black men in the late 1940s. Jefferson, twenty-one and uneducated, has been wrongly convicted of murder and awaits execution at the local courthouse. Grant, in his late twenties, has graduated from university and teaches school in the plantation church house, the only occupation open to an educated black man in rural Louisiana. But it is an occupation that he hates. During Jefferson's trial, the public defender likens his client to a 'hog', an animal not possessed of the intelligence to commit the murder for which he is accused. Coerced by his aunt and Jefferson's godmother, Miss Emma, Grant takes on the duty of 'reclaiming' Jefferson, of sending him to the electric chair a 'man' and not a 'hog' – a label he has begun to accept.

It soon becomes apparent that there are parallels in the lives of these men. Jefferson finds it easier to accept the racist label of the white attorney and the entire white justice system than to challenge it. And Grant has found himself slipping into a pattern of self-loathing and disgust after his six years of teaching. He takes his frustration with a racist system out on his students, threatening to perpetuate the pattern of disregard and hopelessness responsible for the deaths or ruined lives of so many of Grant's contemporaries.

Over the course of a number of meetings in Jefferson's cell, Grant is able to communicate to the younger man the importance of fighting prejudice the only way left to him: by standing tall and rejecting the white definition with pride and dignity. As Jefferson begins to transform under his tutelage, Grant discovers that Jefferson has become the inspirational model missing in his own life. The teacher becomes the student.

Gaines' close character studies explore how this small community of black sharecroppers is tested by Jefferson's impending execution. While it is a symbol for them of their powerlessness in a racist system, it is also a rallying point, a tragic opportunity to express the solidarity of their religious faith and community.

BACKGROUND & CONTEXT

The novel begins in 1947 and ends in early 1948. It takes place in Louisiana, an American state on the Gulf of Mexico between Texas and Mississippi. Louisiana is a very small state, best known for New Orleans, the most famous city on the Mississippi River. Along with the vast territory that came to be known as the Louisiana Purchase, New Orleans was, until 1804, a possession of France (except for a brief period when it was under Spanish control). New Orleans was a major port and was, with the possible exception of New York, the United States' most international city well into the nineteenth century.

Cajun culture

Rural Louisiana was, and remains, a largely agrarian area, that is, one in which cultivation of the land is the main activity. *A Lesson Before Dying* is set on a sugarcane plantation in western Louisiana. Louisiana is also known for its swamps, or bayous, and the culture of people, called Cajuns, who found refuge there and made it their home. The Cajuns were French Catholics who were deported from Nova Scotia, in Canada, when that province was taken over by the English in the late eighteenth century. French settlers had called the peninsula *Acadia*, after the local Indian name, and themselves *Acadians*, a term that eventually became 'Cajuns'. The whites in *A Lesson Before Dying* are Cajun; their French names, such as Pichot, Guidry and Bonin, are an indication of this.

The Cajuns managed to retain much of their culture in Louisiana and many still speak their unique French dialect. Today, most people associate that Cajun culture with their food, such as gumbo and jambalaya, and their music – Zydeco and the fast Cajun fiddle music that is similar to the folk music of Nova Scotia, which comes from the Scottish musical tradition. The Cajuns in *A Lesson Before Dying* are not noticeably different from other American whites of the South during this period, but it is important to realise that they are part of an insular (separate – like an island) community. Obviously, Cajuns have come into some influence in the affairs of Louisiana by the time of the novel, but these French Catholics are in a distinct minority in the predominantly Protestant South.

The Jim Crow South

The Louisiana of *A Lesson Before Dying* is still in the grip of the repressive 'Jim Crow' laws. (Jim Crow was a character in the travelling minstrel shows popular in the South in the nineteenth century.) These laws decreed segregation between whites and blacks and severely restricted the rights of blacks in nearly every aspect of life. They were laws designed to keep blacks 'in their place' – poor, uneducated and disenfranchised (deprived of rights available to others by law).

There is a psychological context in which to contemplate the Jim Crow laws: defeated in and ruined by the American Civil War (1861–1865), Southern whites took out their humiliation on the former slaves whose emancipation resulted from the victory of the North. Every one of these laws, whether designed to repress black education and enterprise, or simply to make life inconvenient – lunch counters, barber shops, phone booths and drinking fountains were all segregated – served to perpetuate the myth that white races are superior to black. This is the legal atmosphere in which Jefferson is convicted of murder – by an all-white jury.

Racial prejudice against Grant Wiggins

The Jim Crow laws reflected a racism that infiltrated all aspects of life: an institutional racism, large, insidious. Witness the humiliations to which Grant is subject every time he mixes with whites, from Sheriff Guidry and Henri Pichot down to the saleswoman at a seedy department store. They all keep him waiting or 'talk down' to him, doing whatever they can to express their perceived superiority. In the society Gaines depicts, blacks face prejudice every day, in endless variation. Yet, of course, racism is also in effect when Grant is away from whites. It lies behind the knowledge that an educated young black man can hope for no higher occupation than teacher in a school neglected by the education board; it is with him in Bayonne, where he is restricted to the black section of town to eat and drink; it is evident in the ruined lives of so many men of his generation.

Segregation and the Jim Crow laws would stand until the landmark civil rights legislation of the 1960s. Of course, the United States still has a long way to go before there is full racial equity, but enormous progress has been made. It is important to understand the *totality* of racism in relation to the time and place of *A Lesson Before Dying*. Although Grant tries to hide from racism by refusing to mix with whites when he can help it, total isolation is impossible. He can avoid neither the more superficial manifestations – the slurs, the indignities at the courthouse, the waiting – nor the deeper consequences of racism.

Sharecroppers and the plantation system

Slavery was a crucial part of the economy of the agrarian South, unlike in the industrial and more populous North. The plain economics of the situation must not be forgotten when one considers the antecedents of the Civil War. Whatever the racist arguments men in power in the South made to defend slavery, this is certain: they knew that if it were abolished, as appeared inevitable with the election in 1860 of President Abraham Lincoln, the entire economic structure of the South would collapse.

The plantation system

The Southern economy depended on the plantation system, on vast farms growing 'money' crops such as cotton, tobacco and sugarcane. Such crops require substantial labour to produce relatively small yields. Under the farming techniques of the 19th century, many hands were needed to pick vast quantities of crop. Plantation owners grew rich because they did not have to pay workers. Slavery was an attractive proposition to them, just as it was to anyone else within the larger economic system surrounding it, such as outfitters, suppliers, buyers, selling agents and transporters. The whole economy of the South depended, and thrived, on slavery. Whites flourished; blacks were treated as chattel. Lincoln's Emancipation Proclamation of 1863 abolished slavery and, with its total defeat in the Civil War, the South was indeed in ruins.

Plantations were generally set up in much the way that Gaines describes in *A Lesson Before Dying*. The main house was the home of the family owning the plantation. Its grandness depended on how large and successful the plantation was. There would also be a series of outlying houses for various uses. Big plantations were basically self-contained communities. They would grow their own food and keep their own animals for work and slaughter. There would be residences for hired white workers – slave overseers, for example – a forge, stables and so on. And, of course, there would be slave quarters. Slaves lived on the plantation and many would never see outside its fences. This is not to say that 'stability' was guaranteed; wives and husbands, parents and children could be split up without notice or consideration when their owners found it expedient to sell slaves.

The plantation of Henri Pichot in *A Lesson Before Dying* is just such a place. The quarter in which Grant and the other blacks live is the old slave quarters of the plantation. Why has so little changed in the more than eighty years between the end of the Civil War and the late 1940s? After the Civil War, slaves were free – but free to go where, to do what? The odds of these former slaves finding their own way to economic prosperity in such a place were nil and, although some of these people migrated to the North and the West, the prospects there held little more promise and many dangers.

Sharecroppers

Not surprisingly, many former slaves returned to the plantations. They became sharecroppers, tenant farmers, provided with housing and equipment by the plantation owners in return for a large percentage of what the sharecropper was able to make out of the land. Many sharecroppers had to do most of their day's work for the plantation boss, with little time or strength left to dedicate to their own bit of land. These people worked their whole lives to pay off the inflated debt that got them started as tenant farmers. In effect, they continued working for the plantation owner with little more than mere subsistence as reward.

Key point

In the worst cases, the lives of sharecroppers were barely distinguishable from their lives as slaves.

There were white sharecroppers, too, but Jim Crow laws ensured that black sharecroppers were denied the kind of mobility available to whites once times improved economically. In *A Lesson Before Dying*, the families who live in the quarter and send their children to Grant's school, with a few exceptions, are sharecroppers. When Grant contemplates the cemetery containing the remains of his ancestors, he is looking back on generations of slaves who became generations of sharecroppers. That the graves of both groups are unmarked and overgrown, merged in anonymity, underscores how little practical difference emancipation made to their lives.

GENRE, STRUCTURE & STYLE

Genre

A Lesson Before Dying is a novel employing a first-person narrative. With one or two notable exceptions, the narrator, Grant Wiggins, writes either about things occurring within the immediate realm of his personal experience or reported to him by others. It is a mark of Gaines' skill that Grant's believability in this role is never stretched. We do not find ourselves asking 'How does he know that?' or winking at his 'luck' in being present to report the proceedings of important conversations. In fact, Gaines' narrator tries at every conceivable juncture to *avoid* his duties, to extract himself from the story entangling him against his will.

Grant's role as unwilling narrator contributes to the novel's realism, evident in its highly detailed portrayal of life on a Louisiana plantation in the 1940s, of segregation and racism, of the boredom and angst of life on death row. Gaines strives to maintain an absolutely realistic representation that is yet riveting. The narrative departs from absolute believability only when Grant writes about events that he has not personally witnessed; for instance, Jefferson's trial (Chapter 1). He takes further liberties in the opening chapter, when he gives a highly detailed account of the killing of the white storekeeper that led to Jefferson's arrest.

But neither of these accounts seems out of place. To begin with, Grant could have received a full report of the trial from any number of people in attendance. The level of detail in Grant's account of the crime seems fully appropriate as well. His narrative reads like the words of a man deeply affected by the story; it has an empathy that turns Jefferson's momentary confusion into a symbol of his plight as an innocent black man at the mercy of a racist judicial system.

The narrative breaks its mould again in the cross-section slice of numerous lives in Bayonne on the day of the execution (Chapter 30). Here the narrative voice takes us into places where Grant obviously did not go. Readers will question whether this is even meant to be Grant's voice at all, or whether it is that of Gaines himself. But the question is largely beside the point. Yes, it could be Gaines momentarily 'taking away' the narrative from his narrator, but it could also be Grant himself writing in a different vein, looking deeply into the lives of the people around him, inventing details, turning the account into art. Either way, the shift in narrative perspective is again linked to a thematic element. This is the day that everyone has been dreading – the day of execution. The narrative shift signals its significance; nothing will be the same again.

Structure

The novel is composed of thirty-one chapters, without any separation into larger units, such as parts. The chapters are relatively short and tend to revolve around a single episode in the story. Gaines has determined that the story, and the responses it is intended to evoke, will best be facilitated by short, dramatic chapters.

Style

A Lesson Before Dying is a realistic novel. Accordingly, the writing style is generally straightforward and unadorned. Gaines does not wish to draw attention to the writing itself but to let the story make its own impact, without trying to lead the responses of the reader through particular stylistic features.

Repetition

An exception is Gaines' occasional use of repetition. In some places he repeats phrases exactly; in other places he repeats syntax. Both types of repetition are used in order to emphasise the emotional state being described at a particular point in the text. Note, for example, the repetition in Grant's description of Jefferson's inadvertent participation in the killing of Mr Gropé:

> He wanted to run, but he couldn't run. He couldn't even think. He didn't know where he was. He didn't know how he had gotten there. He couldn't remember ever getting into the car. He couldn't remember a thing he had done all day. (p.5)

The narrative continues on the next page with an even longer series of simple past-tense sentences beginning with the subject pronoun 'he'. The sentence 'He didn't know what to do' is repeated exactly. The simple form of the sentences emulates Jefferson's state of bafflement after having witnessed the killing of three men within the space of seconds. Nothing makes sense to him. If the entire book were written using this sentence form, it would be unreadable; here, however, it is quite effective. Gaines employs a particular stylistic technique to give the reader access to the character's emotional state.

Social and historical detail

Gaines writes in a very detailed manner at times. Again, this is most often done in the service of realism. We get very close descriptions of people's appearance, of rooms, of food and of routines. For instance, we get an account of every song and speech in the children's Christmas show in Chapter 19. Gaines depicts a world that is totally believable, but there is another purpose behind this use of detail. Consider how many secondary characters there are in *A Lesson Before Dying*; characters such as the beautiful and ill-fated Lily Green (p.248) whose appearance lasts no more than a memorable paragraph. Indeed, Gaines has compiled a cast in this relatively short novel that is almost Dickensian in size. Notice how many characters are introduced and dismissed in Chapter 19 alone.

Such variety and depth of detail should indicate to us that Gaines has made a social and historical commitment in *A Lesson Before Dying* as well as a commitment to tell a story. The world of his novel, the world of the black sharecroppers in rural Louisiana, of the 'quarter', of segregated towns and filthy basement toilets for 'Coloreds' is, thankfully, gone. Gaines is a product of that world, and his novel attempts to be both a document and a tribute. It bears witness to institutionalised racism by cataloguing its practices and consequences, at the same time as it pays tribute to the people trapped by it, preserving something of their lives in the details that Gaines evokes from his memory.

Other stylistic elements to consider

Two other important elements of Gaines' style are the use of dialogue, and variations in the narrative pace throughout the novel.

Q Why does Gaines rely so heavily on dialogue? What purpose do you think it serves?

Q Why are the time intervals between some chapters a matter of hours only, or days, when others are separated by weeks? At what point in *A Lesson Before Dying* does the gap become greatest? Why?

CHAPTER-BY-CHAPTER ANALYSIS

Chapter 1 (pp.3–9)

Summary: Jefferson's trial for murder is described, as is his actual involvement in the crime.

The novel begins with a paradoxical sentence: 'I was not there, yet I was there' (p.3). The unknown narrator, whose identity will emerge in the ensuing chapters, describes the trial of Jefferson, a young black man accused of taking part in the murder of a white grocery-store owner in rural Louisiana in the late 1940s. As the narrator implies in his next sentence, the verdict to be returned by the all-white jury was always a foregone conclusion. Jefferson will be found guilty and sentenced to death. The succeeding description of the crime indicates, however, that Jefferson is innocent of the murder of Alcee Gropé; he had just accepted a ride with Brother and Bear, the two would-be thieves killed by Gropé.

Still, there is no doubt that Jefferson will be convicted: 'A white man had been killed during a robbery ... one [of the killers] had been captured, and he, too, would have to die' (p.4). But it is the words used by the defence attorney in attempting to get Jefferson acquitted that set the 'crisis' of the novel in motion. Denying Jefferson the status of man (though he is twenty-one), the attorney first calls him a 'boy and a fool' (p.7). Three times he intones to the jury members, 'Do you see a man sitting here?' (p.7). Not content with this, he likens Jefferson to an animal, along with all his 'ancestors in the deepest jungle of blackest Africa' (p.7), and a 'thing to hold the handle of a plow, a thing to load your bales of cotton' (p.7). These arguments are made to try to convince the jury that Jefferson was incapable of planning and carrying out the murder; but it is the argument made to keep him from the electric chair that is most offensive: 'What justice would there be to take this life? ... Why, I would just as soon put a hog in the electric chair as this' (p.8).

Key point

This emotive chapter sets the scene for the plot of the rest of the novel. It also establishes one of the novel's main themes: the way in which white people defined blacks, particularly black men, in the American South of the period. Note the terms used to define Jefferson by white men in this chapter. The prosecutor calls him 'animal' (p.6); the defence attorney likens him to a hog (p.8); even Mr Gropé, otherwise kindly disposed towards him, calls Jefferson 'boy' with his dying breaths (p.5).

Chapter 2 (pp.10–15)

Summary: The narrator comes into focus; his aunt and Miss Emma begin to reveal their plan for his visits to Jefferson in jail.

We learn that the narrator, later identified as Grant Wiggins, is a schoolteacher in the 'quarter' of a plantation on the St Charles River in Louisiana (see Background & context). After his aunt, Tante Lou, tells him that Miss Emma wants to speak with him, Grant comes to realise that the two women have unpleasant intentions for him. Miss Emma is Jefferson's godmother (his 'nannan'). An elderly woman who has worked her whole life for the Pichot family, who own a plantation, she is the recipient of as much respect as is possible for a black person in this setting.

Still maintaining the demeanour of pain and detachment that she wore during the trial, Miss Emma says little. Referring to the defence attorney, she says: 'Called him a hog' (p.12). She continues: 'I don't want them to kill no hog … I want a man to go to that chair, on his own two feet' (p.13). Grant realises that Miss Emma wants him to start visiting Jefferson in his jail cell as he awaits execution. His reaction reveals one of Grant's main character traits, cynicism: 'There's nothing I can do anymore, nothing any of us can do anymore' (p.14). In his narrative he shows how much he hates teaching on the plantation and longs to escape.

Chapter 3 (pp.16–23)

Summary: Grant, Tante Lou and Miss Emma drive up to Henri Pichot's house to ask him to intercede with the sheriff to let Grant visit Jefferson.

Henri Pichot is the owner of the plantation. His family would have owned the land and the great house that sits upon it since long before the end of slavery 80 years earlier. The difficulties that the trio has in making the short journey in Grant's car – ruts in the dirt road, a gate that needs opening and closing – serve to reinforce subtly for Grant their subservient status. As Tante Lou says, 'Mr. Henri won't come to him' (p.18).

We learn that Miss Emma had cooked and run the Pichot's house, while Tante Lou did the washing and ironing. As a child, Grant had helped the two women by running errands at the house. When Grant showed an inclination for university, Tante Lou had sent him, telling him that she did not ever want him going through Henri Pichot's back door again: servants use the back door. Though he cruelly throws this back in his aunt's face when he does not want to go to see Pichot (p.17), Grant does not mention the sacrifices that she made for his education or their success – he has not had to go through that back door for many years.

When they see Pichot, Miss Emma makes her request that Grant be allowed to see Jefferson. Pichot tries to talk her out of it in a condescending fashion, but Miss Emma is insistent: 'This family owe me that much, Mr. Henri. And I want it. I want somebody do something for me one time fore I close my eyes' (p.22). Eventually turning his back on her, Pichot returns to the library with his guest and his drink, but not before Miss Emma fires one last remark; it masquerades as a plea, but is really a threat: 'I'll be up here again tomorrow, Mr. Henri. I'll be on my knees next time you see me, Mr. Henri' (p.23).

This chapter introduces us to the complex and depressing protocols of discourse between whites and blacks in *A Lesson Before Dying*:

- Blacks must add 'sir' to statements directed at whites.
- The title 'Mr' must be attached to the first name of any white man to whom blacks refer.

- Whites control conversation, initiating it and deciding when it is finished.

- Blacks are expected to look away when they are finished being spoken to by whites.

Q What is the significance of these 'protocols'? What other ones can we add to the list as we read the novel?

Chapter 4 (pp.24–32)

Summary: *After the meeting, Grant drives into the nearest town, Bayonne, where he has a conversation with Vivian, the woman he loves.*

When the pressures of teaching in the grim quarter get to be too much, Grant escapes to the town of Bayonne, thirteen miles away. Like any other town in the South, Bayonne is divided along racial lines; there is a white section and a 'colored' section. Needless to say facilities such as roads and street lighting are inferior and neglected in the 'colored' section, but Grant feels at home in the Rainbow, a small bar and grill run by the Claibornes. Bayonne is also where Vivian Baptiste lives and teaches. Grant and Vivian are lovers. She has two children from a marriage that she is trying to end. She is having difficulty locating her husband to proceed with a divorce.

Vivian is unselfconsciously beautiful. Grant makes a point of describing the lightness of her skin and the relatively little 'thickness' of her 'nostrils and lips' (p.28). This level of attention may seem strange, but Gaines will use Vivian as a vehicle to explore a kind of colour prejudice that exists among blacks. Later it will be revealed that Vivian's family will have nothing to do with her husband because his skin is much darker than hers, the source of a great deal of pain for her. In other chapters, Grant describes the prejudice of mulattos – people of black and white parentage – in Bayonne. Not accepted by white society themselves, mulattos are equally prejudiced against blacks. In his narrative, Grant very rarely states a person's race, but he almost invariably notes how dark the person's skin is.

Another of Gaines' techniques is evident in this chapter: disclosing important aspects of a character's history or personality through his or her conversation. In Grant's dialogue with Vivian (pp.28–32), we learn about his discontent at the plantation school and his longing to go away with her. We also learn something of their history and of Vivian's inability to leave because of her marriage.

Grant has tried to escape in the past, to his parents in California, but he has returned. It seems that Grant cannot bear to stay at the plantation, yet he cannot stay away. He tells Vivian about Miss Emma's directive that Grant should somehow make a man of Jefferson, complaining: 'Do I know what a man is? Do I know how a man is supposed to die? I'm still trying to find out how a man should live' (p.31).

Key point

This speech shows why Grant is so reluctant to visit Jefferson, but it also suggests that it may be he, more than Jefferson, who is in need of a lesson on living.

Chapter 5 (pp.33–41)

Summary: *This chapter provides a glimpse of life at the school where Grant teaches.*

Grant describes in detail the conditions under which he teaches the children of the quarter. It leaves quite a bit to be desired as a learning environment. The children only go to school for five and a half months out of the year. The schoolhouse is the church; there is one room for all the grades, no desks and few supplies.

Our understanding of this character becomes deeper as Grant tells us about the foul mood that he is in on this day after his meeting at the Pichot house. He takes his frustration out on the children, liberally dispersing corporal punishment for little reason. One might almost blame the 'times' and thus excuse Grant for thinking that hitting children with a ruler is conducive to learning. But the way in which he forces the children to listen to the lurid details of Jefferson's forthcoming electrocution is inexcusably cruel (p.39). He seems to take pleasure in it, callously using the power of his position until one of Jefferson's relations is in tears. His telling the children about Miss Emma's request is grossly inappropriate, unusually lacking in decency for Grant and showing him to be someone on the verge of losing control.

Q Why do you think Gaines shows his protagonist behaving in this way?

Chapter 6 (pp.42–50)

Summary: *Grant is summoned to the Pichot house to meet with Sheriff Guidry.*

Grant is kept waiting for more than two hours in Pichot's kitchen. This is part of the process of humiliation built in to the interactions between whites and blacks. When it was Miss Emma and Tante Lou who had come to see Pichot, he had been a little more timely, though never inviting them to sit down. With Grant, he will exercise his power.

There is an interesting interlude with Edna Guidry, who is the wife of Sheriff Guidry and also Pichot's sister. She comes to see Grant in the kitchen and makes small talk with him, almost as though he were an equal. But it is clear what Edna really thinks of him. Note how she asks Grant to tell her about himself, but stops him: 'No, no need to tell me; I can see you're doing just fine' (p.45). She tells Grant that she would love to have a visit with Tante Lou and that she would like to express her sympathy to Miss Emma, but it is clear that she would never dream of entering the quarter to do so (p.45). She is the kind of white person who likes to think of herself as generous and open-minded to the blacks who serve her. Of course, she is nothing of the sort. When Edna asks Inez, the cook, if there is 'anything that I may help you with' (p.45), it seems unlikely that she can be unaware that the day Inez lets Henri Pichot's sister help serve dinner is the last day she will cook in that house. It is for the reader to decide whether Edna is merely self-deluding or if she is genuinely hypocritical.

Eventually, Grant gets to see the sheriff. He faces a dilemma about his own behaviour: 'Whether I should act like the teacher that I was, or like the nigger that I was supposed to be' (p.47). Guidry does everything in his power to make Grant the 'nigger' rather than the 'teacher', forcing him to go through Miss Emma's request from start to finish, though it is obvious that he has been informed. More importantly, Guidry voices the likely opinion of the entire white community concerning Miss Emma's desire:

> I think the only thing you can do is just aggravate him, trying to put something in his head against his will. And I'd rather see a contented hog go to that chair than an aggravated hog. It would be better for everybody concerned. There ain't a thing you can put into that skull that ain't there already. (pp.49–50)

But Sheriff Guidry does give Grant permission to visit Jefferson at the courthouse.

Chapter 7 (pp.51–8)

Summary: *Grant's school receives its annual visit from the superintendent.*

Obtuse and obese, Dr Joseph cannot remember Grant's name, even after it has been repeated to him. He judges the children by the appearance of their hands and, in some cases, their teeth, reminding Grant of the kind of inspections that potential buyers would make of slaves (p.56). Joseph would be an entirely comical figure if the power he wielded over the education of the children in the quarter were not so ill placed. He will not listen to any of Grant's pleas for more and better supplies, and his suggestions to the teacher that he focus more on flag-drilling and hygiene epitomise the intent of the white authorities to keep the blacks under their control ignorant and compliant.

Chapter 8 (pp.59–66)

Summary: *Grant recalls Matthew Antoine, the mulatto teacher at the schoolhouse when he was a child.*

Grant watches some of the older schoolchildren chop the wood for heating the school, and he thinks about his own days there as a child.

Recalling some of his classmates, he reflects on the violent ends that many of them have met. This leads him to recall the self-hating mulatto teacher of his youth, Matthew Antoine, who had told the children that 'most of [them] would die violently, and those who did not would be brought down to the level of beasts' (p.62). Compared to Antoine, Grant is a capable and decent teacher.

Grant recalls Antoine's advice that the only thing a young black man can do is run. Antoine was a man full of hatred: for the children he taught, to whom he felt superior because of his white blood and the lightness of his skin; for the whites who told him he was inferior; and for himself, because of the fear that made him stay instead of running away. Antoine's declaration that he is 'superior to any man blacker than me' (p.65) touches on the kind of prejudice among blacks noted earlier. When he learns that Grant wants to get an education and later that he has returned to become the teacher, Antoine hates him even more, telling him that nothing Grant does will make any difference. The only reward for Grant's toils will be that the whites will 'make [him] the nigger [he was] born to be' (p.65).

Key point

Antoine represents a kind of 'dark angel' for Grant – a negative model for behaviour. We have already seen some of this model's effects in Chapter 5. The Grant who terrorises and demeans his students is well on his way to becoming another Matthew Antoine, with the same self-loathing and resignation.

Q What does Grant need in his life to keep him from becoming like Antoine?

Chapter 9 (pp.67–74)

Summary: Grant makes his first trip to see Jefferson in his cell at the courthouse.

During the first trip that Grant and Miss Emma make to visit Jefferson at the courthouse, Grant is moody. He is sarcastic about his aunt's and Miss

Emma's demeanours, and overall his narrative conveys a sense of him behaving like a spoilt child who has not been given what he wants. The courthouse itself, a place meant to be the home of justice and equality, is instead a symbol of prejudice and intolerance. Grant notes the statue of the Confederate soldier and the Confederate flag out front, as he will each time he describes the courthouse in the future. The filthy 'colored' toilet is located in the basement. Grant and Miss Emma are subjected to a demeaning search under the instigation of a condescending chief deputy.

Once they get to see Jefferson, they find him sullen and unresponsive. He will not touch the food that Miss Emma has brought him. The reader is struck by the barrenness of his cell as well as by Jefferson's bitterness. His condition makes Miss Emma cry out: 'Oh, Lord Jesus, stand by, stand by' (p.74). It is the young white deputy, Paul, described as looking 'pretty decent' (p.70), who has to suggest, with his eyes, that Grant put his arm around Miss Emma to comfort her.

Chapter 10 (pp.75–9)

Summary: *Grant learns that he will visit Jefferson alone this time.*

Miss Emma feigns illness so that she will not have to see Jefferson. Grant suspects a conspiracy between Miss Emma and his aunt. He becomes very sarcastic and caustic – again, not unlike a spoilt child. He is particularly cruel to Tante Lou, using the words of Matthew Antoine to spite her:

> Years ago, Professor Antoine told me that if I stayed here, they were going to break me down to the nigger I was born to be. But he didn't tell me that my aunt would help them do it. (p.79)

While Grant does have a point about the humiliation he has been exposed to at Pichot's and at the courthouse, his cruelty is unjustified; after all, it has been his aunt's sacrifices that have put him in a position to avoid the humiliation when he so chooses. Tante Lou never had that choice; nor did Miss Emma or any of the others who had to work for the whites. But to make the choice to avoid the humiliation means to hide. Again, we see the figure of 'dark angel' Antoine prodding Grant, trying to make him choose flight instead of facing the world.

Chapter 11 (pp.80–5)

Summary: Grant visits Jefferson alone and finds him belligerent, referring to himself as a hog.

At the courthouse, Sheriff Guidry goes through the ritual of humiliation, making Grant state his intentions for being there, although of course Guidry knows them. Paul, however, actually addresses Grant as an equal. Jefferson is defiant. He goes through a disturbing ritual, on his hands and knees, pretending to eat the food Miss Emma has sent the way a hog would. To Grant's assertion that he is a human being, Jefferson says: 'Youmans don't stay in no stall like this. I'm a old hog they fattening up to kill' (p.83). One gets the impression that Jefferson has been planning this scene, as his initial shock has turned to anger.

Grant tries to motivate Jefferson by telling him that his attitude will 'let [the white man] win' (p.84), but Jefferson remains defiant. Before long, he has turned his face to the wall, ending their discourse. We can see that Grant's task will not be easy. Jefferson's cell is not an environment conducive to trying to convince him that he is not an animal.

Q How effective is Grant's argument about not letting the 'white man' win?

Q Why does Jefferson want to take out his frustration on Grant and his 'nannan'?

Chapter 12 (pp.86–95)

Summary: Grant retreats to the Rainbow to think.

In the Rainbow, after seeing Jefferson, Grant thinks about the nature of heroes. Some men at the bar are discussing Jackie Robinson – the first African-American to break baseball's colour barrier – who had just finished his second year in the major league. The rapture with which these men talk about Robinson leads Grant to think about the idol of his younger years, the great black heavyweight boxer Joe Louis. The emotion with which the blacks of the quarter greeted his knockout of Max Schmeling is the pride of a people desperate for something to be proud of.

These thoughts reflect Grant's current dilemma: he himself could use a Jackie Robinson in his life instead of his Matthew Antoine. Both Robinson and Louis were great athletes who had the added burden of representing their race in a white world. For all those counting on their success, there were many more working for their failure. This is the same situation Grant is in, and he seems well aware that it is a lot easier to be Matthew Antoine than it is to be Joe Louis. His thoughts soon turn to escape again. He seeks out Vivian and goes through what seems to be a kind of ritual with them: he tells her that he wants to escape with her and start over; she responds 'This is all we have, Grant' (p.94).

Chapter 13 (pp.96–102)

Summary: *It is Sunday in the quarter; Tante Lou goes to church; Vivian comes to visit Grant.*

On Sunday, most residents of the quarter go to church. Grant no longer goes, having lost his faith, a cause of friction between him and his religious aunt. While listening to the congregation sing, Grant thinks about the night before, when he returned home late from the Rainbow to find that Tante Lou, Miss Emma and Reverend Ambrose had been waiting for him for hours to hear his report on Jefferson. Grant mentions feeling 'a little guilty' about this (p.98), but that is all. Certainly he does not make the connection readers are apt to make: Grant had considered his wait in Pichot's house an example of the worst kind of intentional humiliation; what is so different about his making Miss Emma wait?

Q Is this an example of his Matthew Antoine side, lording it over those he can, when he can, to assuage his own damaged pride?

Listening to those in church sing their 'Termination songs', Grant reflects on how he lost his faith. What is important about this chapter is not so much Grant's rejection of his religion; rather it is the fact that it troubles him so much. This is due to the fact that religion is always present in the quarter to remind him that he has strayed; it is in his aunt's songs, in Reverend Ambrose's dark looks, in the church where he teaches school every day. It is the background music to daily life, reminding Grant that he is an outsider.

The chapter ends with the unexpected appearance of Vivian at the house. The timing of her arrival suggests that the only thing that Grant has to believe in now is Vivian.

Chapter 14 (pp.103–9)

Summary: Grant shows Vivian his aunt's house; they take a walk around the plantation and make love in the sugarcane fields.

This chapter continues the plot strand of Grant and Vivian's relationship. After having coffee, they go for a walk around the plantation and end up making love, concealed among the sugarcane. They discuss how much they love each other and affirm the fact that they want to have children together. Their having sex without being married seems to be a source of unspoken tension between the two. Vivian is a Catholic and this is 1947. It is hard to determine whether the two are trying to excuse a practice that they think is not quite right by asserting how much they love each other, or whether Gaines himself is doing it. Either way, their conversation about love somehow sounds as much like an apology as a declaration of bliss.

Chapter 15 (pp.110–17)

Summary: Grant brings Vivian back home to meet Tante Lou after church.

Grant determines that Vivian and Tante Lou shall meet. We learn about Vivian's family in Free LaCove, who shunned her when she married a dark-skinned black man. Here we have another case of inner-racial prejudice. This makes things rather complex for Grant and Vivian; we do not know Grant's exact skin tone, but it is to be assumed that he is darker than Vivian. Of course, prejudice like this can work both ways. Perhaps Grant is worried that his aunt will dismiss Vivian as snobbish, simply because her skin is lighter. This concern and the fact that Vivian is still married and the mother of two children make for a nervous meeting.

Tante Lou is not happy about meeting Vivian, but she is very polite. The conflict between Tante Lou and Grant, who feels that his aunt will simply have to accept his love for Vivian, manifests itself not in harsh words or tears, but in the right to make coffee. Grant insists that he will make coffee to replace what he and Vivian drank while the others were at church. Making the coffee in her own house is a right that Tante Lou is not prepared to surrender; she equates Grant's insistence with an attempt to take over her house.

Tante Lou grills Vivian about her family in Free LaCove and their prejudices, and about her religion and its possible conflict with Grant's aversion to religion. The battle between Grant and Tante Lou continues when he has Vivian help him serve the women cake to go with their coffee, another offence against his aunt's domestic authority. Overall, however, Vivian seems to make a good impression; she is judged to have 'quality'.

Chapter 16 (pp.118–24)

Summary: *Grant learns that, during Miss Emma's visit, Jefferson went through the same 'hog' ritual.*

Summoned to see Miss Emma after school, Grant learns that Jefferson had called himself a hog during her visit that afternoon, accompanied by Tante Lou and Reverend Ambrose. They realise that he had lied about his own visit. Thinking that this will signal the end of his visits, Grant is angered when Tante Lou insists that he go back, telling him: 'You ain't going to run away from this, Grant' (p.123).

Chapter 17 (pp.125–34)

Summary: During Grant's next visit, Jefferson shows more anger and tries to bait Grant.

As he is searched by Paul, Grant starts a conversation with the deputy, who continues to talk to Grant without employing any of the techniques whites use to keep blacks 'in their place'. They introduce themselves formally and shake hands. In contrast to this, Grant's and Jefferson's conversation is still full of antagonism, but this time it is not nearly as one-sided as past conversations have been. Grant upbraids Jefferson for hurting Miss Emma so badly on her last visit. In 'teacher mode', Grant says:

> I try to live as well as I can every day and not hurt people. Especially people who love me, people who have done so much for me, people who have sacrificed for me. (p.129)

Q Are Grant's words true? Think about his relationship with his aunt over the past few weeks. Have there been times when he has tried to hurt her?

Jefferson then makes a very insulting remark about Vivian, after first calling her 'that old yellow woman you go with' (p.129). Grant recognises in the remark and Jefferson's look 'the expression of the most heartrending pain I had ever seen on anyone's face' (p.130). Jefferson is lashing out against the only people he can, out of his deep pain. We have witnessed this already in Grant, a condition he has learnt from his 'dark angel', Matthew Antoine.

On his way out, Grant is sent to see Sheriff Guidry. It seems that Miss Emma would like to meet Jefferson in the dayroom, a place where all of them can sit down, from now on. This story is most notable for the reappearance of the hypocrite Edna Guidry, who has been pressuring her husband to accede to Miss Emma's wish. During a visit by Miss Emma, Tante Lou and Reverend Ambrose, she set the precedent of having her maid serve them coffee before getting down to business. When Miss

Emma begins making demands on her, Edna Guidry develops a splitting headache, and badly bungles the meeting with an insensitive remark (p.133).

Chapter 18 (pp.135–41)

Summary: *This chapter depicts the next visits by Miss Emma and the others, and then by Grant.*

Miss Emma meets Jefferson in the dayroom of the courthouse, but he remains sullen and uncooperative, not eating any of her food. During Grant's next visit, Jefferson again refers to himself as a hog. It is becoming apparent that he does this for reasons beyond simple bitterness; it seems to be a kind of defence mechanism for Jefferson. If he adopts the role of 'hog' in which the white authorities have tried to cast him, Jefferson will not have to care about himself any longer and will be able to disassociate himself from the terrible thing that is being done to him. His ubiquitous comment 'Don't matter to me' (p.139) is evidence of this disassociation. Having lived his entire life in an environment in which he is told over and over that he is insignificant and inferior, Jefferson takes a perverse kind of shelter in the idea – he is not a 'youman', so why should it matter if he is going to be killed?

Key point

Jefferson's attitude is an extreme example of something about which Grant himself is so concerned: the acceptance by blacks of the labels that whites put on them. In Grant's terminology, it is being made 'the nigger he was born to be'. This is the essence of the defeatism and resignation in someone like Matthew Antoine. If *A Lesson Before Dying* is about anything, then it is about the necessity of rejecting such definitions.

Chapter 19 (pp.142–51)

Summary: *The school Christmas pageant.*

In attendance at the children's Christmas pageant is a cross-section of the quarter. Gaines' brief profiles, from Bok, the mentally challenged young man, to Miss Rita, to James Lavonia, another prejudiced mulatto, with 'better things to do than go to a coon gathering' (p.145), show his writing at its best. Bit by bit, he creates a community out of what seem insignificant details. Indeed, the identity of the community is in such details, in that they demonstrate what a community is: an association of individuals. The individuality of the people of the quarter is exactly what the whites who exploit them are not willing to recognise. One of the adhesives keeping this community together is a strong faith. The lines spoken by one of the children in the nativity play, 'The lowest is highest in His eyes' (p.149), reveal the essence of the faith of a people who have little other evidence of the manifestation of divine grace.

But as with any community, some people are excluded. Reverend Ambrose's thinly disguised attacks on Grant's agnosticism (belief that nothing can be known or proved about the existence of God) indicate the requirements of membership. The chapter ends with the following assertion in Grant's narrative: 'I looked back at the people around the tables, talking, eating, drinking their coffee and lemonade. But I was not with them. I stood alone' (p.151).

This statement echoes the opening sentence of the novel: 'I was not there, yet I was there'. In both cases, Grant is talking about an absence or presence existing beyond the physical, that has to do with his problematic identification with the community of the quarter.

Q How important is the issue of Grant's 'belonging' to the community in understanding this character and the novel?

Chapter 20 (pp.152–9)

Summary: *A date is set for Jefferson's execution; Grant is summoned to Pichot's house to receive the news.*

The news everyone in the quarter has been dreading arrives. That dread is perfectly reflected in the defeated posture of Farrell Jarreau, who comes to tell Grant the news and summon him to the big house (p.153). This time, the meeting takes place in Pichot's sitting room rather than in the kitchen. Consider how ironic it is that the first time black people from the quarter are bestowed such an honour is to mark the finalisation of the unjust execution of one of them.

The furniture in this room, faded and from a dead era, is metaphoric for the Pichots and others like them – white landholders trying to keep alive the inequity and repression of the slave era years beyond emancipation. The governor has set a date for the execution soon after Easter, but not so soon as to offend Louisiana's many Catholic voters (p.156). The cynicism of this manoeuvre prompts Grant to recap in his mind just what an offence against justice the whole process has been; a black man in the wrong place at the wrong time, convicted by an all-white jury uninterested in his side of the story, is now to be killed at the convenience of the state (pp.157–8). In considering the nearness of the date to Easter and the fact that the execution is to take place on a Friday, Grant recalls Christ, another innocent man sacrificed to the status quo.

Chapter 21 (pp.160–7)

Summary: *The quarter turns out to visit Miss Emma, who has taken to bed after hearing the news.*

Vivian comes to see Grant upon hearing the news and they go to visit Miss Emma. Grant had stopped in earlier, having made sure that he did not have to be there when Miss Emma was told that the date had been set. Needing a drink, Grant and Vivian drive into Bayonne and settle themselves in the Rainbow. Vivian voices some rather out-of-character jealousy regarding Irene Cole, one of the older children whom Grant uses to help teach the younger ones. This gives Grant an opportunity to explain to her the source of some of the pressure he feels from the community: 'The rest of them love me, too, and don't want an outsider taking me away from them. They want me for their own … because they have so little' (p.165).

Grant explains that Irene and his aunt want the same thing from him that Miss Emma wants from Jefferson: to stand for them, to break the 'vicious circle' in which black men, unable to shoulder the burden placed on them by 300 hundred years of slavery and repression, run away. Because of his education, and his ability to teach, Grant appears to them as the only 'unbroken' man, who 'can give them something that neither a husband, a father, nor a grandfather ever did, so they want to hold on as long as they can' (p.167). But this too is part of the circle: 'Not realizing that their holding on will break me too. That in order for me to be what they think I am … I must run as the others have done in the past' (p.167). This sums up at least one of Grant's dilemmas: the pressure placed on him to succeed by those who love him.

Concluding the chapter, Vivian asks Grant if the circle will ever be broken. Grant responds: 'It's up to Jefferson' (p.167).

Q Is this true? Is it up to Jefferson alone? Do you think Vivian was asking Grant about Jefferson, or about Grant himself?

Chapter 22 (pp.168–77)

Summary: Grant makes his first visit to Jefferson after the execution date has been set.

At the courthouse, Grant is submitted to the ritual of being searched by the deputy before being admitted to see Jefferson. Clearly, Paul does not want to search Grant. But Clark, the chief deputy, looks on to ensure that the search is carried out. Here the 'new' Southern white man, tolerant, open, willing to treat Grant as an equal, is contrasted with the 'old' Southern white man, bigoted and eager to take any opportunity to humiliate Grant.

During the visit, Jefferson opens up a little to Grant and they have some normal conversation, free of belligerence or baiting. Jefferson talks about eating a whole gallon of ice cream for his last meal. He calls it his 'last supper', again making the association with Christ. We are reminded of the innocence of this young man, not just with regards to the killing of Mr Gropé, but to life itself. After leaving Jefferson, Grant buys him a radio at Edwin's department store, where the white saleswoman does everything in her power to demonstrate to Grant his lowly position (p.176). Sheriff Guidry does the same when Grant takes the gift to the courthouse.

Chapter 23 (pp.178–86)

Summary: *There is a confrontation between Grant, his aunt and Reverend Ambrose over the radio; Grant makes his next visit.*

When Miss Emma, Tante Lou and Reverend Ambrose next visit Jefferson, he does not come down to the dayroom because he does not want to leave his radio. They go up to his cell, but the visit is a disaster. Miss Emma turns the radio off, which makes Jefferson retreat into himself. Later that day, Grant is confronted by his aunt and Reverend Ambrose, neither of whom can see the radio as anything but an incitement to sin. To them, anything but church music comes directly from the devil. Grant says that if they take away the radio, he will not visit Jefferson any more (p.183). It is clear that a battle is brewing between Grant and Reverend Ambrose over the direction to be taken in the reclamation of Jefferson before his execution.

During Grant's next visit to the courthouse, he and Jefferson talk about music on the radio, but little else until Jefferson tells him to thank the 'chirren' for the 'pe-pecans' (p.186) that Grant has brought with him. Grant is filled with joy, as this is the first time that Jefferson has seemed to be able to get outside the cell of his own bitterness to consider how much the community of the quarter is supporting him. They shake hands at parting, another first, signalling that they are beginning a new phase in their relationship (p.186).

Chapter 24 (pp.187–194)

Summary: Grant accompanies Miss Emma and the others on their next visit; he tells Jefferson what he would like from him.

The tension between Grant and Reverend Ambrose continues during the next visit. Paul is not at the courthouse, so they are led to Jefferson by Clark, the bigoted chief deputy. He stops in the restroom and makes them wait five minutes just to show them that he is in charge (p.188). Jefferson will not eat any of the gumbo that Miss Emma has made, so Grant takes a little walk alone with him in the dayroom to try to coax him into it. He asks Jefferson to eat some gumbo to show Miss Emma that he loves her.

Grant then outlines what he would like to achieve with Jefferson. He tells Jefferson that he has the opportunity to be a hero to the quarter by being 'above other men' (p.191). Jefferson can be a hero in a way that the self-loathing Grant or the bullying Reverend Ambrose never could – by doing something unexpected and standing tall. This would be a great gift to the community, even as it defies the whites who want and expect a complacent 'hog' to go to the chair: 'To them, you're nothing but another nigger – no dignity, no heart, no love for your people' (p.191).

Key point

Grant tells Jefferson that he can help to break the myth of superiority to which the whites are clinging. Finally, he tells Jefferson that he needs him, much more than Jefferson needs Grant. In essence, Grant is telling Jefferson how desperate he, Grant, is for a Jackie Robinson – a hero as role model, someone to break the spell of Matthew Antoine. Jefferson can be that for Grant and for the community.

Grant is essentially asking the same thing of Jefferson that he said was being asked of him by his aunt and by Irene and the others of the quarter – the same thing that he has said would break him or drive him away.

Chapter 25 (pp.195–203)

Summary: *Grant gets into a fight with two mulatto men at the Rainbow.*

This chapter returns to the issue of inner-racial prejudice. Grant tells us about the mulattos, who will take on almost any kind of work to avoid 'working side by side in the fields with the niggers' (p.198). Two bricklayers at the Rainbow talk loudly enough in disparagement of Jefferson that Grant challenges them to fight, despite his having entered the bar elated because Jefferson had eaten some gumbo for Miss Emma.

Though described in realistic detail, the real purpose of the fight in this novel is metaphoric; it displays the inter-black prejudice, fed by self-hatred, that tears the community apart. It also reminds us of Grant's contemporaries who died in bar fights just like this one. Even Grant, armed with his education and his determination not to let himself be destroyed by the system, can find himself fighting nearly to the death with other black men. This violence is frustration speaking. It is the desperation of black men hitting the only target they can – themselves.

Chapter 26 (pp.204–10)

Summary: *Grant and Vivian discuss the fight.*

Vivian is very angry about the fight. When Grant tells her that he simply could not take it any more, she responds: 'That's how you all get yourselves killed' (p.206). This reinforces the point made above, about how frustration and humiliation manifest themselves in violence in the black community. But Vivian is also condemning Grant for not showing self-restraint. To an earlier suggestion of hers, that he should have simply left the bar, Grant responds: 'Can Jefferson walk out of where he is?' (p.205). This is not the first time that Grant has equated his plight with Jefferson's.

Key point

The previous chapter ended with an extended exchange about whether Grant could stand up after his fight (p.203). In this chapter, the issue of whether Grant can stand up at Vivian's place also becomes important. Knowing that Grant is determined to get Jefferson to 'stand up like a man' before he goes to his execution, we might conclude that the fight had been some kind of test of manhood for Grant. If so, Vivian obviously thinks that he has failed: a man does not fight and get himself killed in a bar over a trifle; he 'stands up' by walking away, by doing anything to avoid jeopardising the position of the woman he loves.

They argue over the issue, and it leads to a dangerous moment in which they question their entire relationship. Grant seems to be on the point of leaving forever at the end of the chapter, but he returns, knowing that Vivian is the only thing in the world that he loves.

Q Is Grant justified in comparing his plight to Jefferson's? How is Grant's experience in the Rainbow similar to Jefferson's caged existence in the courthouse? How does it differ?

Chapter 27 (pp.211–18)

Summary: Grant has a serious discussion with Reverend Ambrose.

The struggle between Grant and Reverend Ambrose finally comes to a head in a private discussion. This exchange begins with Reverend Ambrose seeming as tyrannical and inflexible about God and religion as we might expect. He says that he will fight Grant with all the strength of his body, if necessary, not to let him send Jefferson's soul to hell (p.215).

By the end of the chapter, however, we come to know him a little bit better. Reverend Ambrose feels deeply in the debt of his community, not because of their respect for him, or for the fact that they support his church, but for the strength of their belief in God and that some day there will be relief from their terrible burdens. He reproves Grant, saying that he is not 'educated' for all his schooling. This is because Grant does not recognise that to relieve suffering is his job, even if it means lying, and that the history of their people in the quarter is a history of lying to oneself, sacrificing truth in order to keep hope alive.

Reverend Ambrose wants Grant to help him to help Jefferson find God before his execution; in this he is a kind of adversary, because it requires Grant to convey ideas that he does not believe in, like the existence of heaven. It remains to be seen whether Reverend Ambrose's desire for Jefferson's redemption and Grant's resolve to see him defy white prejudice by standing tall are compatible.

Chapter 28 (pp.219–25)

Summary: Grant has his penultimate meeting with Jefferson.

On the day before Good Friday, Grant visits Jefferson. They talk about the significance of Easter and Jefferson makes a connection between Christ's death ('without a mumbling word') and his own, to come in two weeks' time. They discuss Reverend Ambrose and, as feared, Jefferson asks Grant about his own beliefs. Grant says that he is lost, but that Jefferson's and Miss Emma's beliefs are important. One of the things that Reverend Ambrose has told Jefferson, about having to give up 'worldly possessions', is shown by Jefferson to be empty: 'what on earth I got to give up, Mr. Wiggins?' (p.222). When Grant talks about doing something for Miss Emma, about making sacrifices, Jefferson asks what sacrifices have been made for him and if anyone would be willing to go to the electric chair in his place. He concludes: 'No, Mr. Wiggins, I got to go myself. Just me, Mr. Wiggins' (p.223). Again we are reminded of Christ, taking on the burdens of humanity alone.

A little later, Jefferson outlines his dilemma: how is he to be 'better than ever'body else' (p.224) when all his life he has been told, by whites and blacks alike, that he is no more than an ignorant servant? He went to work at the age of six, after being abandoned by his parents. He has known nothing but hard work and hard words, yet now he is being asked to become something bigger in death – to carry a cross.

This strikes a deep chord in Grant, who seems now truly to believe in what he has been telling Jefferson: 'My eyes were closed before this moment, Jefferson. My eyes have been closed all my life. Yes, we all need you. Every last one of us' (p.225). These are similar words to those used by Reverend Ambrose in the previous chapter. It is almost as if the apostate (revered leader) has come back to his religion.

Chapter 29 (pp.226–234)

Summary: *This chapter is composed of entries by Jefferson in the notebook that Grant gave him.*

You may find it difficult to read this chapter, but it will be rewarding to persevere. This is Jefferson in his own voice, not responding to anyone's prompts – Grant's or Miss Emma's or Reverend Ambrose's – as he has done to this point. He comments on his life and asks metaphysical questions about why God seems to favour the whites and the rich (p.227). He recalls Boo, the drunk and defiant non-believer, lying on the road and tempting God to strike him (p.228).

But it is the way in which Jefferson relates the events that occur in the two weeks after Grant's last visit that are most interesting. He is deeply touched by the visit of the children to his cell (p.230). The generosity of Bok, who gives him one of his marbles, the only things that he prizes in life, makes Jefferson cry. He makes peace with his nannan, telling Miss Emma that he is strong and that he loves her (p.231). He cries again, learning Grant will not see him on his last day, saying that Grant is the first person to make him feel like somebody (p.232).

Some of the white characters make their appearance in Jefferson's journal as well. Sheriff Guidry cynically tries to persuade Jefferson to write something good in his journal about his treatment (p.233). Here Guidry seems to be trying to assuage his conscience. One of the worst qualities of oppressors of any colour is the way they convince themselves of their beneficence to those they repress. Even more cynical is the visit by Pichot and Mogan, who discuss their bet about whether Jefferson will go to the electric chair a man or a hog (p.229). Undoubtedly, this is the only reason why they came.

Jefferson's final entries show a man understandably frightened, but determined to conduct himself as well as he can.

Chapter 30 (pp.235–45)

Summary: This chapter covers the morning of the execution.

This chapter is composed of vignettes, or small sketches, of moments in the lives of various people, some of whom we are meeting for the first time, on the morning of Jefferson's execution. Gaines is giving us another view, similar to the one in Chapter 19, into the lives of ordinary people. The only point of connection is that each somehow comes into contact with the electric chair as it passes through town, or with Jefferson himself. Here again, Gaines' writing shines.

There is an interesting contrast on page 237. Reverend Ambrose prays to God for the strength that he knows he will need as a witness. Sheriff Guidry prays that everything goes smoothly during his first execution. The thoughts of many of the whites in town are well summarised in the ugly comments of the clerk at the bank on page 242. The vignette in which Jefferson is shaved by one of the other inmates (pp.243–5) is riveting. It slows down the action in writing stripped of everything but straightforward description, yet somehow Gaines manages to instil amazing suspense in the scene. It ends with Paul, the only remotely sympathetic white figure, promising Jefferson that he will be there when the time comes.

Chapter 31 (pp.246–56)

Summary: Grant talks about his actions on the day of the execution.

Grant has determined that he will not be there to watch Jefferson die. He admires the bravery of Reverend Ambrose (p.249), but knows that he himself does not have the strength. Grant has decided that he will have his students get on their knees and pray for Jefferson from midday until they hear from the courthouse that the execution has taken place. When the time comes, he walks out into the quarter. It is quiet, as none of the black sharecroppers are working that day, out of respect for Jefferson.

Grant asks himself: 'Why wasn't I there … Why wasn't I back there with the children? Why wasn't I down on my knees?' (p.250).

Key point

This is the question that Grant has been alluding to from the beginning of the novel. Grant is in the community, but not with them. He is separate, even though he shares their anguish exactly.

The answer to Grant's question comes on the next page, when he says: 'Don't tell me to believe' (p.251). He is referring to the God in whom the whites find justification for their prejudice and injustice. But, he realises, the blacks of the quarter must believe: 'if only to free the mind, if not the body' (p.251). Their faith is the only thing that allows them to transcend their circumstances. It gives them the strength to face the inequity and hope for something better. Grant concludes that, bereft of that faith, he himself is a slave to the bitterness that threatens to destroy the good works that he is capable of performing.

An emblematic butterfly appears, lighting on a patch of bull grass 'that offered it nothing' (p.252). Grant wonders why this is so, and his question prompts us to see faith and hope lighting on the community of the quarter, despite its seeming hopelessness. Perhaps we might also see the dignity visited upon Jefferson in his last hour, and consequently upon the rest of the community, in this little harbinger of spring and metamorphosis.

As if in response, Paul drives up and tells Grant that it is over, and that 'He was the strongest man in that crowded room' (p.253). He tries to convince Grant that he must be a great teacher, because the transformation in Jefferson from the defeated and ignorant boy to the 'strongest man in that room' has been remarkable. Paul has been deeply touched. He leaves Grant, saying: 'Allow me to be your friend, Grant

Wiggins. I don't ever want to forget this day. I don't ever want to forget him' (p.255). The butterfly suggests the possibility of something new in Louisiana, a chance at equity, as demonstrated by people like Paul, who are willing to stick out their hand to people like Grant.

A Lesson Before Dying ends with Grant returning to his class to face his students. We suspect that there will be a change in his teaching and in his commitment to them from this day on. In the 'lesson' implied by the novel's title, Grant has also been a pupil.

CHARACTERS & RELATIONSHIPS

Grant Wiggins

Key quotes

'I was not there, yet I was there.' (p.3)

'I had told [Tante Lou] I was no teacher, I hated teaching, and I was just running in place here.' (p.15)

'I need to go someplace where I can feel I'm living ... I want to be with you [Vivian], someplace where we could have a choice of things to do.' (p.29)

Vivian: 'You went to California to visit your mother and father – but you wouldn't stay. You couldn't stay.' (p.30)

'Do I know what a man is? Do I know how a man is supposed to die? I'm still trying to find out how a man should live.' (p.31)

'I had come through that back door against my will ... but I damned sure would not add hurt to injury by eating at [Pichot's] kitchen table.' (p.46)

'I tried to decide just how I should respond to [Pichot and Sheriff Guidry]. Whether I should act like the teacher that I was, or like the nigger that I was supposed to be.' (p.47)

Guidry: 'You're smart ... Maybe just a little too smart for your own good.' (p.49)

'Professor Antoine told me that if I stayed here, they were going to break me down to the nigger I was born to be. But he didn't tell me that my aunt would help them do it.' (p.79)

Vivian: 'You know the answer yourself, Grant. You love them more than you hate this place.' (p.94)

'I have always done what they wanted me to do, teach reading, writing, and arithmetic. Nothing else – nothing about dignity, nothing about identity, nothing about loving and caring ... And I went along, but hating myself all the time for doing so.' (p.192)

'There was nothing outside [Vivian's] house that I cared for ... not anything else in the world.' (p.210)

Reverend Ambrose: 'They sent you to school to relieve pain, to relieve hurt – and if you have to lie to do it, then you lie.' (p.218)

'My faith is in you, Jefferson.' (p.249)

The protagonist of *A Lesson Before Dying*, Grant Wiggins, in his late twenties, has been the teacher at the plantation schoolhouse for six years. He says that it is the only job available for an educated black man in rural Louisiana. The opening of the novel finds him hating his job, hating where he lives and, though he does not say it, hating himself. He talks constantly about running away, but he cannot do so. This is the source of his greatest dilemma. He cannot bear to be where he is, but he knows that it is the place where he belongs.

His aunt, Tante Lou, has helped to raise him, and has worked hard and sacrificed to send him to university. He has been once to visit his parents in California. His parents had left the plantation during World War II, when Grant was around twenty years old. Now, Grant is back on the plantation, hating it, but unable to leave it. Devout Tante Lou is disappointed by his rejection of religion. They maintain an adversarial relationship throughout the course of the novel. The same is true of his relationship with Reverend Ambrose, the local preacher, who sees Grant as, at best, a lost soul and, at worst, an agent of the devil.

But Grant's real problems have to do with his calling. His hatred for the plantation stems from his understanding of the racism upon which it depends. He cannot stand to see the many ways in which whites, such as Henri Pichot, Sheriff Guidry, the public defender in Jefferson's trial and Dr Joseph, repress the blacks on the plantation. Yet he feels powerless to fight this prejudice.

Grant is not a revolutionary; he would rather avoid the whole situation by simply keeping clear of the whites when he can. The fact that he is more offended by the humiliation to which his visits to Jefferson subject him than by Jefferson's sentence indicate just how self-centred he is about racism. His education has given him the tools to understand racism, but, at the novel's beginning, he is only concerned with how it affects him. This has isolated him from his community. Grant looks at his students and, angered by how little has changed since his own childhood, he takes it out on them, instead of trying to change things.

We see this most clearly in Chapter 5, but the isolation that Grant feels from his community is evident throughout the book. Think of the number of variations on its opening sentence: 'I was not there, yet I was there'. Grant is a man on the margin, 'betwixt and between'. As the most educated man on the plantation, the teacher of the school, he should be one of the leaders in a community desperate for them. But he is marginalised by his contempt. Its ugliest manifestation is an urge to follow the path of Matthew Antoine, hating his students for reminding him of his inferior status.

Matthew Antoine had said that if Grant stayed there long enough, the whites would make him 'the nigger he was born to be'. Suffering the humiliations of Pichot's kitchen and Sheriff Guidry's courthouse, Grant is certain that this is indeed happening to him. But he does not realise that the worst danger does not lie in such treatment. To become Matthew Antoine, to hate his students and lash out against the blacks in the quarter is a far worse fate than suffering humiliation. Following that path is truly to become the whites' 'nigger', for nothing better supports the apparatus of racism than inter-black hatred.

Key point

This is really the main challenge faced by Grant: to reject Matthew Antoine and find a new model of behaviour.

Grant takes refuge from these difficult choices in Vivian, though their relationship is not without problems (see below). She ends up being instrumental in turning him towards the right path, due to the strength that he derives from her love. But he also tends to associate Vivian with avoidance and the easy answer; he is constantly asking her to 'run away' from Louisiana and start anew. This side of Grant may not be quite as bad as his Matthew Antoine side, but Vivian knows that it is wrong, and she resents the fact that Grant associates her with his urge to quit.

In the end Grant seems reformed. The 'lesson' in the book's title is really one given to him. While Grant has been trying to instruct Jefferson about dignity, it is Jefferson who teaches him what it really means in his last weeks on earth. Upon hearing Paul Bonin's account of Jefferson's death at the end of the book, Grant cries before heading back to the schoolhouse to tell the children. This indicates that he has finally learnt the vital importance of showing courage in the face of the impossible. Matthew Antoine would not cry in the same situation; he would sneer. Though doubts remain in Grant's mind about his future on the plantation, it is not another Matthew Antoine returning to that classroom.

Jefferson

Key quotes

'He wanted to run, but he couldn't run. He couldn't even think. He didn't know where he was. He didn't how he had gotten there.' (p.5)

Defence Attorney: 'Gentlemen of the jury, look at this – this – this boy. I almost said man, but I can't say man.' (p.7)

Defence Attorney: 'Why, I would just as soon put a hog in the electric chair as this.' (p.8)

'All the same ... It don't matter.' (p.73)

'Youmans don't stay in no stall like this. I'm a old hog they fattening up to kill.' (p.83)

'His expression remained the same – cynical, defiant, painful.' (p.84)

'I recognized his grin for what it was – the expression of the most heartrending pain I had ever seen on anyone's face.' (p.130)

'Easter when they nailed Him to the cross. And he never said a mumbling word.' (p.139)

'How do people come up with a date and a time to take life from another man? Who made them God?' (p.157)

'I want me a whole gallona ice cream.' (p.170)

Grant: 'As long as none of us stand, they're safe. They're safe with me. They're safe with Reverend Ambrose. I don't want them to feel safe with you anymore.' (p.192)

Grant: 'You – you can be bigger than anyone you have ever met.' (p.193)

'What about me, Mr. Wiggins? What people done done to please me?' (p.222)

'That's how I want to go, Mr. Wiggins. Not a mumbling word.' (p.223)

'i jus cant sleep no mo cause evertime i shet my eyes i see that door.' (p.228)

'an i jus set on my bunk cryin … cause they hadn never done nothin lik that for me befor.' (p.231)

'i tol [Miss Emma] i was strong.' (p.231)

'i got to be a man an set in a cher.' (p.234)

Paul: 'He was the strongest man in that crowded room.' (p.253)

Jefferson is an uneducated young black man of twenty-one, wrongly convicted of murder and awaiting execution in the courthouse in Bayonne. Abandoned by his parents as a child, he has been raised by his nannan, Miss Emma. But nothing in his upbringing, or in his treatment by the whites, for whom he began working at the age of six, has led Jefferson to believe that he was good for anything but menial labour. Over the course of his visits to him, Grant witnesses an enormous change in Jefferson's emotional state, from mute shock to anger and belligerence, to bitter resignation, to a hesitant altruism (unselfish concern for others) and, finally, to strength.

Jefferson is a kind of test case of prejudicial labelling. He has been likened to a 'hog' by the bigoted public defender assigned to his case. The central conflict of the novel is whether Jefferson will accept this label and go to the electric chair meekly or violently or ignorantly – that is, in any fashion that the whites would associate with a hog – or whether he will go 'like a man'. It is Grant's task to try to effect the latter possibility. But, for Jefferson, the choice is more difficult. Early after his conviction and sentencing, Jefferson hides in the 'hog' persona as a way to escape, or at least to avoid his fear and indignation.

Key point

Jefferson has never been told that he is anything more than an animal. It is easy for him to accept the status that the whites have been forcing upon him all his life.

This dilemma, whether Jefferson will 'live down' to the white definition, or whether he will challenge it by showing dignity, is shared by Grant (see above) and, Gaines seems to imply, by all blacks. Will they allow their identity, their very sense of themselves, to be dictated by the prejudice of whites or will they define it for themselves? Blacks 'living down' to the definitions of the whites (see Themes & issues) are found in many contexts in the novel: in Jefferson's initial acceptance of the role of 'old hog'; in Matthew Antoine's hatred of himself and the students over whom he feels superior; in the bigotry of Vivian's light-skinned family in Free LaCove; in Grant's resentment against his students; in all those contemporaries of his killed in bars or languishing in prison for manslaughter.

Jefferson's relationships with other characters reflect his growth from the introverted and hostile young man in a cell to the generous, proud man who walks to the electric chair. His diary (Chapter 29) offers an interesting look into his mind.

Vivian Baptiste

Key quotes

'I'm still married ... I can't go anywhere until all this is over with.' (p.29)

'Yes, Grant, you would hate me for letting you make this decision [to flee together]. Or I would hate you for doing it.' (p.141)

'That's how you all get yourselves killed [Grant's fight in the Rainbow].' (p.206)

'I heard from him [her husband] ... He won't give me a divorce unless he can see his children every weekend.' (p.208)

Beautiful and kind, Vivian is separated from her husband, but not divorced. She is the mother of two children and, fearing that her husband will demand custody, she is unwilling to do anything to jeopardise her position. This creates a source of tension between her and Grant, who would like to leave Bayonne with her. Unlike Grant, Vivian truly feels called to the profession of teaching; she wants to improve the community in any way she can. And unlike him, she has a very strong faith. She loves Grant, but not the side of him that wants to run away, nor the side that compels him to take out his frustration on his students. Grant's love for

Vivian creates an opportunity to express his negative aspects, particularly the desire to escape. But this love also highlights Grant's positive side, giving him strength to keep trying to instil in Jefferson a sense of identity and dignity.

Readers might see Vivian as little more than a foil for Grant. Her bigoted family in Free LaCove and the difficulties of her separation offer some complication to her character. However, besides a spell of very uncharacteristic jealousy, involving the child Irene Cole, Vivian is near perfect. This makes her conspicuously unlike the other flawed and realistically drawn characters.

Tante Lou

Key quotes

'Of course, it pained my aunt to see this change in me, and it saddened me to see the pain I was causing her.' (p.102)

'She really knew how to be polite to people when she felt they were interfering with something that belonged to her.' (p.163)

'She wanted to cry. And she wanted to slap me. Not only for this moment, but for all those years that I had refused to go to her church.' (p.182)

'That's how you got through that university – cheating herself here, cheating herself there, but always telling you she's all right.' (Reverend Ambrose to Grant, p.218)

Tante Lou is a very powerful figure in Grant's life and she acts as an adversary to him in the novel for a number of reasons. Key among them is the fact that Grant no longer accompanies her to church. She is a devout Christian, and his apostasy has deeply hurt her. But there are other things about Grant that Tante Lou does not like: his cynicism, his sarcasm, his reluctance to help Miss Emma and Jefferson. She seems unwilling to let go of Grant, to admit that he is a man and able to make his own decisions. Her cold welcome to Vivian in Chapter 15 testifies to this. There is no question that Tante Lou is a strong-willed, domineering, inflexible person, but her role as antagonist to Grant can make us forget her foremost qualities: self-sacrifice, determination and generosity.

Tante Lou raised Grant's mother, her niece, when her sister left the plantation, and then she raised Grant when his mother and father left during World War II. Tante Lou is the one who stays, the one who makes sure that the children are raised properly when their parents leave them behind. She has worked under humiliating circumstances, as laundry woman in the Pichot's house, longer and harder than she needed to, so that Grant could go to university – and so that he would never have to go through the Pichot back door again. The way in which Grant throws this sacrifice back in his aunt's face justifies her disappointment in him. Tante Lou is determined to stand by her best friend, Miss Emma, in her time of need, rarely leaving her side.

Reverend Ambrose

Key quotes

'He stared at me as though I was one of the worst of sinners.' (p.101)

'The Lord don't hate you, Sister Emma ... The Lord is with you this moment. He is only testing you.' (p.123)

'No matter how educated a man was (he meant me, though he didn't call my name), he, too, was locked in a cold, dark cell of ignorance if he did not know God in the pardon of his sins.' (p.146)

Grant: 'I'm not going back down there and tell her he's going to die April eighth. Not me.'

Reverend Ambrose: 'You'd have the strength if you had God.' (p.158)

'[Jefferson] ain't got but five more Fridays and a half. He needs God in that cell, and not that sin box [radio].' (p.181)

'This is a mean world. But there is a better one. I wish to prepare him for that better world.' (p.214)

'I won't let you [Grant] send that boy's soul to hell ... I'll fight you with all the strength I have left in this body, and I'll win.' (p.215)

'You think a man can't kneel and stand?' (p.216)

'I know my people. I know what they gone through. I know they done cheated themself, lied to themself – hoping that one they all love and trust can come back and help relieve the pain.' (p.218)

Reverend Ambrose is the spiritual leader of the blacks of the plantation. He has had no formal seminary training; one day he heard the 'calling' and became a preacher. He has a strong belief in God and is dedicated to helping those who share his belief. His sense of debt to the people in his flock, for their sacrifice, their humiliation and their longing for relief, is genuine (see Chapter 27). But Reverend Ambrose is contemptuous of those who do not share his belief, or follow all of his prescriptions. Another complicated figure, Reverend Ambrose encapsulates both the positive and negative characteristics of the very devout. He is nearly as constant as Tante Lou in support of Miss Emma, yet he sees nothing wrong in belittling Grant for his disbelief. He supports Jefferson on the day of his execution, yet he would take away the one thing that makes him happy, his radio, because it is a 'sin box'.

Grant detects envy in Reverend Ambrose when he, Grant, is able to get Jefferson to eat some of Miss Emma's gumbo (Chapter 25). There is a kind of competition going on between the two men for Jefferson's mind and soul. While Grant wants Jefferson to 'stand up' in pride and dignity before he dies, Reverend Ambrose wants him to find God at any cost. His comment 'You think a man can't kneel and stand?' (p.216) reveals Reverend Ambrose's belief that earthly dignity is available only to those who have first humbled themselves before God. Because Grant has rejected this belief, Reverend Ambrose sees him as something like an agent of the devil.

Miss Emma

Key quotes

'Oh, yes, she did hear one word – one word for sure: "hog".' (p.4)

'She knew, as we all knew, what the outcome [of the trial] would be.' (p.4)

'Her large, dark face showed all the pain she had gone through this day … No. The pain I saw in that face came from many years past.' (p.13)

'I don't want them to kill no hog … I want a man to go to that chair, on his own two feet.' (p.13)

'Somebody got do something for me one time 'fore I close my eyes.' (p.22)

> 'I'm sorry, Mr. Grant, I'm helping them white people to humiliate you ... And I
> wished they had somebody else we could turn to. But they ain't nobody else.'
> (p.79)

> 'I don't know if Miss Emma ever had anybody in her past that she could be
> proud of ... But she wants that now, and she wants it from him [Jefferson].'
> (Grant, p.166)

Emma Glen, the godmother of Jefferson, has worked most of her life for the Pichots as cook and housekeeper. She is a figure of great respect and dignity in the quarter. The catalyst for the main action of the novel, she is more powerful than she appears or pretends to be. She can get relatively strong male figures, such as Pichot, Sheriff Guidry and Grant, to do things they do not want to do – to a point. While it is interesting to note the subtle manipulation in her 'He don't have to go' (Chapter 10) concerning Grant's visits to Jefferson, or her canniness in using Edna Guidry as an intermediary with the sheriff, what little power Edna has comes from her many years of sacrifice.

It is in women like Miss Emma and Tante Lou that the community of the quarter finds its pride, rather than in the men who leave or are broken in one way or another by white prejudice. This is truly a sad statement, not because Miss Emma's perseverance and determination are not admirable, but because such respect is *only* given – grudgingly by the whites – to women who have given their lives in menial service to white families. Still, in Miss Emma and Tante Lou is also to be found the strength of the community, personified in their resolve and their self-sacrifice.

Paul Bonin

Key quotes

> 'Paul nodded. He understood. He had come from good stock.' (p.140)

> 'Allow me to be your friend, Grant Wiggins. I don't ever want to forget this
> day. I don't ever want to forget him.' (p.255)

Paul is the lone sympathetic white character. He is recognised by the blacks as being of 'good stock' – in a similar way that Vivian is recognised as possessing 'quality'. He seems as bothered as Grant is by the ritual of examining Miss Emma's food every time they come to the courthouse. This suggests that Paul understands something about racism that the other whites do not: that its practices are demeaning both to the target and the perpetrator. Although Paul does not want to get too close to Jefferson, he is clearly sympathetic before the execution, and he is deeply moved afterwards by Jefferson's dignified demeanour. Paul introduces himself to Grant as though the other is an equal, and he offers him his friendship at the end of the book.

Paul is the future, a small spark of white tolerance and humanity. We can see this by contrasting him with the chief deputy, the racist Clark, who makes Grant wait while he uses the toilet. While that spark of humanity has not exactly blazed into an inferno in American race relations, the Clarks have lost their public support; they now mutter in the dark rather than act brazenly in the light. Whites like Paul would play important roles in the civil rights struggles to begin not long after the time of A Lesson Before Dying.

Sheriff Guidry

As one of the chief agents of a deeply racist system of government, Guidry is bigoted, condescending and self-important. There is no reason to conclude that Guidry the man is any different from Guidry the sheriff. He is willing to allow some flexibility in considering Miss Emma's requests regarding visits to Jefferson, but he will not let humanitarian interest interfere either with his duty as sheriff or his standing as the 'man in charge'. He uses the tactic of humiliation liberally with Grant, not simply because Grant is black, but because he is educated and the sheriff is not. Again, this is Guidry the man behaving, reminding Grant that as a white man he is superior, regardless of his rank as the head of the police.

Henri Pichot

Henri Pichot is the last of the Pichots to live in the ancestral house on the plantation on St Charles River. His family has owned the place, and the slaves on it, for generations. The blacks living there may no longer be slaves, but not much else has changed. Pichot does whatever he can to maintain a master–slave relationship with his sharecroppers and servants. He is rarely presented without a drink in his hand, a symbol subtly indicating that there is nothing much of merit in his life; he has no children and, it seems, few entertainments besides food and drink. He does not like Grant, and he keeps him standing in his kitchen to prove it. He shows some deference to Miss Emma, but when one considers that she likely did more to raise him than his own mother, that deference can only be called parsimonious (mean).

Matthew Antoine

A self-hating, prejudiced mulatto, Matthew Antoine was the teacher at the school when Grant was a child. He is a Creole, a term that has a variety of meanings, depending on cultural context. In this case, it means that Antoine is probably of mixed Hispanic or Caribbean and African ancestry, something that sets him more apart from the sharecropper culture than the other mulattos in the novel. He is Grant's 'dark angel', the negative role model, advising that Grant flee rather than try to make a difference at the plantation. He is a perfect example of what can happen when rage and hatred, abetted by cowardice, are turned inward. Because of his illness, he never feels warm. We can see this condition as an extension of the coldness of his soul.

The Claibornes

Joe and Thelma are the older couple who run the Rainbow bar and café. They are kindly disposed to Grant – although Joe knocks him out during

Grant's fight with the mulatto bricklayers – and are willing to lend him money or give him a meal on credit.

Inez

Inez has succeeded Miss Emma as cook and housekeeper at Pichot's. She is distraught when Pichot and the sheriff keep Grant waiting more than two hours in the kitchen, repeatedly offering him food or coffee.

Edna Guidry

Edna is Henri Pichot's sister and Sheriff Guidry's wife. She typifies the white hypocrite who *thinks* that she is being open and fair to the blacks, even as she lives comfortably within a racist society. She intercedes with her husband on behalf of Miss Emma in the matter of visits to the dayroom with Jefferson. But the cost is a 'splitting headache' and moments of panic when the blacks, to whom she has shown the unprecedented courtesy of a chat in her parlour, do not act with the anticipated deference.

Dr Joseph

The white school superintendent, Dr Joseph cannot remember Grant's name from year to year. He is one of the faces of institutionalised white prejudice. Under his stewardship, the education department makes sure that the black children do not have enough or the correct supplies; that the school year is shorter for them than for the white children; that they will not learn anything but to accept the racist status quo.

Irene Cole

One of the older girls at the school, Irene teaches the younger children for Grant and helps generally with lessons. She is idealistic and intelligent; she wants to be a teacher. Irene is a model of what the next generation of the quarter *could* be, but her devotion to Grant makes him see her as another representative of the expectations that are suffocating him.

THEMES & ISSUES

Racism

The environment of 'institutionalised racism' depicted in *A Lesson Before Dying* has been touched on in Background & context. It is important to distinguish between the racist beliefs held by individuals and those held by institutions, such as legislators, judiciaries, public enforcement agencies and school boards. These views may, of course, be identical, but their effects are quite different.

The following illustration will help to clarify this. The public defender assigned to Jefferson uses a racist argument. We can abhor or dismiss the man as a racist, knowing that such people exist; in so doing, we have made a decision about him as an individual. But the novel also compels us to consider the degree to which this defender is playing his role in a racist system – the Louisiana judiciary. From the twelve white men on the jury to the prosecutor, to the public defender, and no doubt to the judge, the bailiff, even the court reporter – we know that the whole system is founded on racist beliefs.

Key point

Racist beliefs are so entrenched that Grant does not even bother to attend the trial; he knows, as does everyone else, what the verdict will be and what the sentence will be.

Gaines gives us enough glimpses into the psychologies of his white characters for us to judge the degree of their racism. Upsetting as their actions and opinions may be, the black characters deal with them as best they can. Again, the opinions of Sheriff Guidry, Henri Pichot or the saleswoman at Edwin's may reflect the racism of the system at large. But it is the institutionalised racism that does the most damage in the lives of the African-Americans of the quarter and living in Bayonne.

Lack of opportunity

As Grant tells Jefferson, there is nothing for an educated black man to do in rural Louisiana but teach in the local plantation school. It goes without saying that this is a job without hope of advancement. Although Grant deeply resents this situation, he is one of the 'lucky ones'. Think of the schoolmates he writes about, the ones who left the quarter because there was nothing for them, only to find worse lives, early death, or life sentences in the state penitentiary at Angola – which remains the most notorious prison in the United States. Jim Crow laws and the institutionalised racism that they personify have ensured that black men have few options. They can wander, looking for work that does not exist, or they can stay, and become little more than beasts of burden like Jefferson. Either way, the atmosphere is a great incentive either to hopelessness or the recklessness that devolves out of hopelessness.

Identity

The theme of identity in *A Lesson Before Dying* intersects with the issue of institutionalised racism. Of course, the plot revolves around the question of Jefferson's sense of identity. It is Grant's task to get Jefferson to see himself as a *man*, rather than as the 'hog' he is likened to by the public defender. These comments go to the heart of racism, for racism is nothing other than the refusal to see other humans as humans, based on imposed classifications of what it *means* to be human.

During the slavery period in the United States, slaves were considered to be property in legal terms: the same rules that applied to a white person's ownership of a bullock or a mare applied to their ownership of a slave. In *A Lesson Before Dying*, set eighty years after the abolition of slavery, whites still regard blacks as animals. And this view is still a cornerstone of the institutionalised racism that will send Jefferson to the electric chair for a crime that he did not commit.

Furthermore, the whites in *A Lesson Before Dying* use such racist doctrine – indeed, require it – to define *themselves*. Consider to what extent the self-image of whites is determined by their relationships with blacks, from the saleswoman at Edwin's, to the bank clerk, to the hypocritical Edna Guidry, to Henri Pichot. Each uses racism as a way to raise his or her self-esteem; no matter how devoid they are of power, status or influence, they are at least better than the blacks who wash their clothes, and whom they can keep waiting as long as they like.

The most distressing thing for Miss Emma is when Jefferson himself accepts the racist equation, calling himself a hog during her early visits to his cell at the courthouse. Later, in his diary, Jefferson likens himself to a workhorse, raised for nothing but mindless labour. This is the most daunting problem facing Grant: how is he to make a man out of someone raised and 'educated' to think that he is good for nothing more than the work of an animal? While an individual's racist opinions can harm only to a certain extent, institutionalised racism can influence how men and women of the targeted group think about *themselves*. What Grant is trying to fight in Jefferson's initial acceptance of the 'hog' label is exactly this – a skewed and defeating self-definition that is the product of hundreds of years of slavery and Jim Crow. It is the creation of an environment in which every interaction with whites every day reinforces his alleged inferiority and uselessness.

Grant's sense of identity

Grant too must struggle with his sense of identity. Matthew Antoine had warned Grant that somehow the whites would make him the 'nigger he was born to be'. Antoine is Grant's 'dark angel', the negative role model to whom we can attribute most of Grant's negativity about his job and his position. Antoine's advice to Grant is flight, because Grant could never make a difference staying on in the quarter. In the early stages of his meetings with Jefferson, Grant sees the petty humiliations that he suffers at the hands of people like Pichot and Guidry as exactly what Antoine had warned him about – they are indeed trying to turn this educated and intelligent young man into the 'nigger he was born to be'. Grant's solution up to this point has been to hide. He has taken Tante Lou's dictum, that he never go through Pichot's back door again, too far. Not having the courage to flee and make a new life somewhere else, he has settled on hiding in the quarter, avoiding the humiliations associated with contact with whites.

By doing this, Grant is becoming what the whites want him to be. He is becoming another Matthew Antoine, a bitter, self-loathing individual who tries to boost his own ego by lashing out at those unfortunate people within his power – namely, the children of the school.

Key point

Grant is succumbing to the racist model: armed with the tools to help make a difference, he is actually maintaining the status quo.

This all has to do with the way in which Grant sees himself. Just as he must break Jefferson's identification with the public defender's 'hog', so too must Grant break his own identification with Matthew Antoine. It is only when Grant actually realises the power that Jefferson might have – to give hope to his community by giving them pride in the man who transcended the unjust sentence imposed upon him – that he begins to identify the power with which he himself might enact change.

A quote from murdered South African rights activist Steve Biko is relevant here: 'The most potent weapon in the hands of the oppressor is the mind of the oppressed'. Gaines makes the relevance of Biko's sentiments most apparent in characters like Matthew Antoine and the black-on-black racism that defines them. There is little question that Gaines condemns this form of racism as strongly as he does white-on-black racism.

The fight between Grant and the racist mulattos, the prejudice of Vivian's light-skinned family, Matthew Antoine – these are all examples or outcomes of that destructive self-defining seen in Jefferson's initial adoption of the animal identity placed upon him by the public defender. Oppressors turn the minds of the oppressed into weapons by tricking them into adopting and internalising the oppressor's definitions of them. This is the Matthew Antoine urge – the voice of the 'dark angel' telling mulattos that they are better than 'blacks' (even though they are still 'black' to the whites), telling Jefferson that he is an 'old hog', telling Vivian's family that they are better than dark-skinned blacks, telling Grant that the children he teaches will never amount to anything.

Education

Another theme in the novel concerns education, and what the term really means. Grant is, of course, a teacher. It would be interesting to count up the number of times that a character says something like the dismissive 'you're the teacher' when Grant is nonplussed about something. He is treated with deference by most of the blacks of the quarter because of his university education, but it is equally an inducement to scorn, particularly from the whites. It is a difficult situation. Grant is expected to have all the answers; worse, he is expected to lead. Reverend Ambrose takes him to task for his apostasy from the faith he preaches; Miss Emma expects him somehow to make Jefferson a man; Vivian expects him to remain in the quarter and make a difference in the lives of the children he teaches; Sheriff Guidry expects him to ensure that Jefferson remains compliant. These pressures are placed on Grant because of his education and because he, in turn, is an educator.

But Grant is lost, uncertain of his skill and calling, trapped by self-doubt and harmful self-definitions. Reverend Ambrose makes a very strong point when he tells Grant that he, Reverend Ambrose, is the educated one because he knows his people and tends to them, while Grant is a 'gump' who only thinks about himself. It becomes apparent, at least by the middle of *A Lesson Before Dying*, that it is the 'teacher', Grant, who is arguably most in need of the lesson in the title. But this issue of what it means to be educated, or to educate, will not so easily be resolved. And Gaines does not lead our conclusions. We know at the end of the novel that his experience with Jefferson has deeply affected Grant, and we can feel reasonably sure that Grant will become a better teacher. One of the 'lessons' he seems to have learnt is that real wisdom is to be found in unexpected places. But how will he apply what he has learnt from Jefferson to his classroom? How will he provide a real education for those children when they have no reason to associate education with any kind of meaningful outcome?

These are difficult questions, but Gaines is telling us that they need to be answered before society can proceed. It is only in education that we have any hope of defeating racism and other prejudices. Does this mean that formally educated people cannot be prejudiced? Hardly. But a true education requires expansion of the mind.

Key point

To educate oneself means to question the labels that people impose from the outside. This is without question one of the novel's key points.

Heroism

A Lesson Before Dying also makes us think about the meaning of the term 'heroism'. Grant reflects on how his community is in desperate need of heroes. He remembers a chilling story concerning a young black man being dragged to the electric chair, pleading: 'Please, Joe Louis, help me' (p.91). In Grant's youth it was Joe Louis; at the time of the novel, it is Jackie Robinson, whom everyone in the quarter is talking about and whom blacks all over the United States are holding up as their hero. Before moving on to heroism within the action of *A Lesson Before Dying*, it is worth considering the kind of pressure placed on Joe Louis and Jackie Robinson. It is difficult enough to become an elite athlete, but imagine excelling at a game as difficult as baseball when you are the only black person. Imagine being subjected to racial taunts and threats at every ballpark you play in – from the opposing players as well as the spectators.

Many people can excel under positive conditions, but *heroism* occurs under conditions of crisis and duress. These terms certainly apply to Jefferson's situation. Awaiting his execution, he is being asked by Grant to do something that no-one would ever have imagined possible from him, even under the most favourable conditions: to stand up like a man and, by standing up, to strike a blow against the racism responsible for his impending death.

Q Can we say the same thing about Grant? Is he in a situation where he can choose to act heroically?

Q What about the other characters? To what degree can we say that characters like Tante Lou, Miss Emma, Vivian and even Reverend Ambrose act heroically?

Fight or flight

These seem to be the two options in Grant's life. He talks constantly of leaving the quarter forever and seeking a new life, perhaps in California where his parents are. The other option is to stay on and do his best to fight the racism and the negative self-defining and despair that accompany it. The latter is, of course, Vivian's preference – she is dedicated to making things better – and it seems, at the end of the novel, that Grant will stay on.

We do not learn much about Grant's parents. We know that they left the quarter during World War II, looking for opportunity, but we learn little else. Grant went to visit them in California once, but he soon returned; we do not know why. As readers, we do not really know what to think of these parents. Are they bold pioneers or are they quitters? We are never given a frame of reference with which to make a decision. All we know is that they have left, and they would be crazy to come back. The war era was a time of great mobility and, paradoxically, opportunity in the United States. Many African-Americans left their rural lives to occupy newly created jobs in cities. This exodus played a dramatic role in redefining black identity, which in turn played an important part in the civil rights movements to come.

The 'fight or flight' issue boils down to this: the novel seems to be telling us that Grant's mission in life is to stay on the plantation and teach its children – to stay and 'fight', if you like. But we might ask: what is *wrong* with his desire to go somewhere else? Is he not entitled to try to

make the best life for himself that he can? Is it not more appropriate for
him to join his parents in California than to stay on with his great aunt in
racist Louisiana? Where is the shame in fleeing such a place? Arguably,
Gaines intentionally makes the issue opaque; after all, life rarely hands
us clear choices. Still, without knowing any more than we do about his
parents – in other words, without being supplied a reason why he should
not join them – Grant's fight or flight dilemma might seem imposed and
rather artificial.

Q How do you respond to Grant's parents' move to California?

Justice and capital punishment

A Lesson Before Dying offers strong arguments against capital punishment.
The United States remains one of the very few industrialised, Western
nations to still use the death penalty. In the late 1940s, most of those nations
still had the death penalty, Australia included, but Gaines' accusation is
directed squarely at current times. The percentage of minorities executed
continues to be grossly disproportionate to their representation in the
general population. This is also true of the general prison population.
While the justice systems of Southern states in the US have improved
since the time of *A Lesson Before Dying*, institutionalised racism persists,
and it plays an undeniable role in convictions and sentencing. Some
people make the argument that capital punishment is indeed little more
than a tool of institutionalised racism.

There is also great disparity in convictions and sentencing between
socioeconomic classes. Poor men and women like Jefferson are still
receiving incompetent representation from randomly assigned public
defenders. That is not to say that the great majority of these attorneys are
not motivated and honest, but often their preparation time is negligible,
as is their access to possibly exculpatory evidence (that is, evidence that
results in a not guilty verdict). Once again, it is the minorities, blacks in
particular, who are most likely to require a court-appointed defender.

There are those who say that there are two kinds of justice in the United States – white justice and black justice.

Whether through racism, incompetence or indifference, the United States justice system remains deeply flawed. The trial that Jefferson receives in *A Lesson Before Dying* is grossly unfair. Gaines' novel indirectly makes the argument that unfair trials continue to exist today – particularly if the defendant is a young black man accused of killing a white man or woman. Mistakes can be made; justice can be subverted – but executions cannot be taken back.

QUESTIONS & ANSWERS

This section focuses on your own analytical writing on the text, and gives you strategies for producing high-quality responses in your coursework and exam essays.

Essay topics

1   "I was not there, yet I was there." Discuss Grant Wiggins' relationship to the community of the plantation quarter.

2   "I recognized his grin for what it was – the expression of the most heartrending pain I had ever seen on anyone's face." How do Jefferson's reactions to his impending execution change?

3   "Of course, it pained my aunt to see this change in me, and it saddened me to see the pain I was causing her." Discuss the relationship between Grant and Tante Lou.

4   "Allow me to be your friend, Grant Wiggins." What role does Paul Bonin play in the novel?

5   "Do I know what a man is? Do I know how a man is supposed to die? I'm still trying to find out how a man should live." Describe the central dilemma in Grant's life.

6   "i got to be a man an set in a cher." 'A Lesson Before Dying explores heroism and the many forms it can take.' Discuss.

7   "That's how you [Grant] got through that university – cheating herself here, cheating herself there, but always telling you she's all right." How does A Lesson Before Dying explore the importance of self-sacrifice?

8   "I know my people. I know what they gone through. I know they done cheated themself, lied to themself – hoping that one they all love and trust can come back and help relieve the pain." What role does faith play in the lives of the people of the quarter?

9   "What you see here is a thing that acts on command. A thing to hold the handle of a plow, a thing to load your bales of cotton, a thing to dig your ditches, to chop your wood, to pull your corn." In what ways is Jefferson's life shaped by the racism practised in the South in the first half of the twentieth century?

10   "I tried to decide just how I should respond to [Pichot and Sheriff Guidry]. Whether I should act like the teacher that I was, or like the nigger that I was supposed to be." How does the novel explore the connection between racism and self-identity?

Analysing a sample topic

"I tried to decide just how I should respond to [Pichot and Sheriff Guidry]. Whether I should act like the teacher that I was, or like the nigger that I was supposed to be."

How does the novel explore the connection between racism and self-identity?

Look closely at the question and consider exactly what it is asking. It is not asking for a general assessment of racism in *A Lesson Before Dying*; it is asking you to address a particular aspect of racism – namely, the way that it influences self-identity. All questions have an element of suggestion, an indication of what teachers or examiners are looking for. In this case, the quote from Grant is clearly prompting you to consider the way he sees himself and to what degree that has been influenced by the racist society in which he lives.

Ask yourself some questions to further examine this idea. Is Grant the only one whose self-perception is influenced by racism? What about Jefferson? A very strong case can be made for this character as well. Look even deeper. The racism in *A Lesson Before Dying* permeates every aspect of life, every segment of the population.

If you really think about it, you could probably assess, at least briefly, how each character's self-identity is influenced by racism. Some other fertile possibilities are: Matthew Antoine, Tante Lou, Vivian. But do not forget the white characters. Is not their self-image greatly influenced by the racism that they practise? Consider again the quote used in the question. Grant is trying to determine how he should behave in front of two powerful and deeply racist white men. I would suggest that their expectations of Grant's behaviour have everything to do with their *own* self-image. Racists define themselves by their beliefs about the inferiority of other races.

Having considered the many possibilities for examples, narrow your list to three or four at the most. You want to be able to give due consideration to individual examples, rather than discuss so many characters that you cannot actually say much about any.

Next, create a brief outline of your essay. Decide which character you will discuss first, and organise the argument into about five or six main points. Do the same for the other characters.

Determine what the order of your overall argument will be. Remember, you have to do more than simply look at how individual characters' self-identity have been affected. You are expected to make a cohesive argument. After you have considered examples of characters' self-image in relation to racism, develop a strong contention, that is, your main argument.

Your essay will be structured like this:

- The introduction should include your contention while incorporating some of the specific arguments that you intend to make about individual characters.

- The body of your essay will look at the individual characters that you have decided to discuss, but always with an eye on your main contention. Demonstrate the depth of your knowledge of the book, but do not stray from the line of argument that you have initiated.

- Your conclusion should revisit some of the major points that you have made, but it should not just repeat them. A conclusion is an opportunity for you to demonstrate what the reader has learnt from your discourse. A good essay is not a circle; it is a spiral.

SAMPLE ANSWER

"I went up to the desk and turned to face them. I was crying."

How does Grant progress from cynicism to a realisation that running away does not solve either his or his people's problems?

At the end of the novel when the white deputy sheriff tells the first-person narrator 'you're one great teacher, Grant Wiggins', Grant realises for the first time that he has the talent to make a difference for his people. A black teacher for black children in southern Louisiana in the 1940s, Grant is cynical about the efficacy of his work in a white supremacist society where black skin denotes low social status and means being a victim of ongoing oppression. Painfully, Grant learns that running away from a problem only continues to generate the cycle of social injustice, and that one man can make a difference.

When Miss Emma, the matriarchal figure of the black quarter on a plantation near Bayonne, recruits Grant to 'teach' her godson, Jefferson, to become 'a man', he unwillingly assumes the responsibility. Jefferson has been wrongly convicted of murdering a white man and is sentenced to death. His court-appointed defence lawyer, instead of calling witnesses, relies on the established white view that, as a black man, Jefferson is subhuman and therefore incapable of planning and carrying out a conspiracy to murder. This appeal to social Darwinian theory results in Jefferson being called 'a hog' rather than 'a man' but, nevertheless, fails before an all-white jury. Miss Emma wants Jefferson to go to his execution with pride in himself and pride in his race. Grant sees this not only as impossible, but also as a pointless task. University-educated in California, Grant's high ideals – that he can help his students overcome the racial prejudice that dominates their lives – have been eroded in the face of the ongoing subjugation of his people. The words of his own teacher echo in his ears; that is, that most of the educated blacks would either die violently or 'be brought down to the level of beasts'.

Grant's anger and frustration at a system he fears will never change make him a reluctant advocate for Jefferson, who continually rebuffs his attempts to elevate his spirit. But Grant is educated enough to understand that Miss Emma is seeking a more profound outcome than merely helping Jefferson. This is her last chance 'to see a black man stand for her' in a matriarchal community where 'we black men have failed to protect our women since the time of slavery'. She wants the vicious cycle of abandonment in the face of prejudice to be broken. Grant, too, is in danger of repeating the cycle as his grandmother and parents had done before him, and it is only his love for another black teacher, Vivian Baptiste, that has kept him pursuing his 'duty' in the face of despair. These women want dignity restored to a proud race that has been subjugated because of economic self-interest, fear and ignorant prejudice.

Grant has little time for the organised religion that Tante Lou and Reverend Ambrose represent, but when Jefferson begins to show just how perspicacious he is, Grant feels 'like someone who had just found religion'. His impassioned plea to Jefferson that he has the power to break the prevailing white myth that blacks are only 'three-fifths human' is deeply moving. When Grant asserts that he 'needs' Jefferson to show him what to do with his own life, that Jefferson 'can be bigger than anyone' because of his unique opportunity to make a heroic sacrifice, Grant shows his own enlightenment. In convincing Jefferson that there is a higher ideal to strive for, he sees his own way more clearly.

Because Jefferson goes to his execution 'the strongest man in that crowded room', Grant is able to recognise his own part in Jefferson's transformation. When he turns to face his students 'crying', Grant acknowledges that the 'lesson before dying' is that no-one can escape their commitments and their ties to those that love them. Change can be wrought only by those who make a 'stand' against injustice and prejudice.

REFERENCES & READING

Text

Gaines, Ernest J 1998, *A Lesson Before Dying*, Hodder Headline, Sydney.

Further reading

Gaines has written seven other novels: *Catherine Carmier, Of Love and Dust, Bloodline, The Autobiography of Miss Jane Pittman, A Long Day in November, In My Father's House* and *A Gathering of Old Men*. Each of them has the same setting as *A Lesson Before Dying*, in and around the invented town of Bayonne in western Louisiana.

Interview

Ferris, B 1998, '"I heard the voices … of my Louisiana people": a conversation with Ernest Gaines', *Humanities*, July/August, Vol. 19 No. 4, https://www.neh.gov/humanities/1998/julyaugust/conversation/i-heard-the-voices-my-louisiana-people